SPORTS
ALL-ST★RS

EZEKIEL ELLIOTT

Jon M. Fishman

Lerner Publications ◆ Minneapolis

Lerner Publications Company
A division of Lerner Publishing Group, Inc.
241 First Avenue North
Minneapolis, MN 55401 USA

For reading levels and more information, look up this title at www.lernerbooks.com.

Main body text set in Albany Std 15/22. Typeface provided by Agfa.

Library of Congress Cataloging-in-Publication Data

Names: Fishman, Jon M., author.
Title: Ezekiel Elliott / Jon M. Fishman.
Description: Minneapolis : Lerner Publications, 2018. | Series: Sports All-Stars | Includes bibliographical references and index. | Audience: Age 7–11. | Audience: Grade 4 to 6.
Identifiers: LCCN 2017019222 (print) | LCCN 2017022340 (ebook) | ISBN 9781512482638 (eb pdf) | ISBN 9781512482478 (lb : alk. paper) | ISBN 9781541512023 (pb : alk. paper)
Subjects: LCSH: Elliott, Ezekiel, 1995-—Juvenile literature. | African American football players—Biography—Juvenile literature. | Football players—United States—Biography—Juvenile literature. | Running backs (Football)—United States—Biography—Juvenile literature.
Classification: LCC GV939.E46 (print) | LCC GV939.E46 F57 2018 (ebook) | DDC 796.332092 [B]—dc23

LC record available at https://lccn.loc.gov/2017019222

Manufactured in the United States of America
1-43296-33116-9/12/2017

CONTENTS

LION
KILLER

Ezekiel Elliott streaks down the field in a December 26, 2016, game against the Detroit Lions.

Dallas Cowboys running back Ezekiel Elliott is strong. He's fast. And when he gets the football in his hands, he knows what to do with it.

Elliott put all his skills on display in a game against the Detroit Lions on December 26, 2016. If the Cowboys could win, they would tie their all-time record for wins in a season. The game was tied in the first quarter when Cowboys quarterback Dak Prescott handed the ball to Elliott on the Dallas 45-yard line.

Elliott dashed up the middle of the field. He blasted through the Detroit **defensive line**. He was in the clear! Elliott cut to his right

Ezekiel Elliott (left) made his jumping dive into the end zone ahead of Detroit Lions player Glover Quin.

and turned on his world-class speed. A Detroit defender almost caught up with him as the running back neared the **end zone**. But there was no stopping Elliott. At the 5-yard line, he leaped and stretched in the air. Elliott crossed into the end zone. Touchdown!

The fans in Dallas roared with excitement. Elliott danced for the crowd. Then his teammates caught up with him to celebrate. "Whenever we're out here with this team, we have fun," Elliott said later.

Dallas fans knew that Elliott was a fast runner. But many still marveled at the incredible speed he showed during the touchdown run. He streaked down the field at more than 21 miles (34 km) an hour. No wonder the Lions couldn't keep up!

Elliott led the Cowboys with 80 rushing yards during the game against the Lions.

Elliott's touchdown put the Cowboys ahead by seven points, but the game wasn't over yet. Detroit scored the next two touchdowns to wrestle the lead away. With the Lions ahead, 21–14, Dallas wide receiver Dez Bryant caught a 25-yard touchdown pass. At halftime, the game was tied, 21–21.

The second half was all Dallas. Detroit had the ball first, but quarterback Matthew Stafford threw an **interception**. A few plays later, Elliott cruised into the end zone for his second touchdown of the day. The Cowboys kept piling it on. They added two more touchdowns to make the final score Dallas 42, Detroit 21.

Elliott (*left*) celebrates a touchdown with teammate Joe Looney.

In addition to being a fierce runner, Elliott is good at catching passes.

Elliott was one of the most exciting players in the NFL (National Football League) during the 2016 season. But Dallas fans hope the best is still to come. After all, 2016 was Elliott's first year in the league. He is ready for the challenge. "This is what I've worked my whole life for, and I wouldn't have it any other way," he said.

Ezekiel's football success started when he was young. In high school, he was invited to play in a special US Army All-American Bowl game.

Ezekiel Elliott was born on July 22, 1995, in Alton, Illinois. He grew up with his mother and father, Dawn and Stacy Elliott, near St. Louis, Missouri. Ezekiel has two younger sisters, Lailah and Aaliyah.

The University of Missouri is sometimes called Mizzou for short.

Ezekiel has always loved to play sports. As a child he would find a way to play, no matter where he was or what he was doing. "[He] used to ball up a pair of socks to make a ball," his mother said. "If he didn't have a ball to play with, he'd make one."

He got his love of sports from his parents. They both went to the University of Missouri. Stacy played **linebacker** for the football team. Dawn was a track-and-field star who competed in the **heptathlon**.

Ezekiel attended high school at John Burroughs School in St. Louis. He played basketball and competed in track and field. He also racked up more than 4,800 rushing yards for the John Burroughs football team and scored an incredible 90 touchdowns.

Elliott got offers to play at more than 20 different colleges but chose to attend Ohio State University.

With so much success in high school, Elliott received offers from some of the country's top college football teams. They all thought the powerful runner could be a star. Since both his parents had gone to Missouri, Elliott almost followed in their footsteps. But instead, he chose Ohio State University. "This is the biggest decision I've ever made," he said. "It's heartbreaking because I'll always love Missouri. But I just think Ohio State is a better fit."

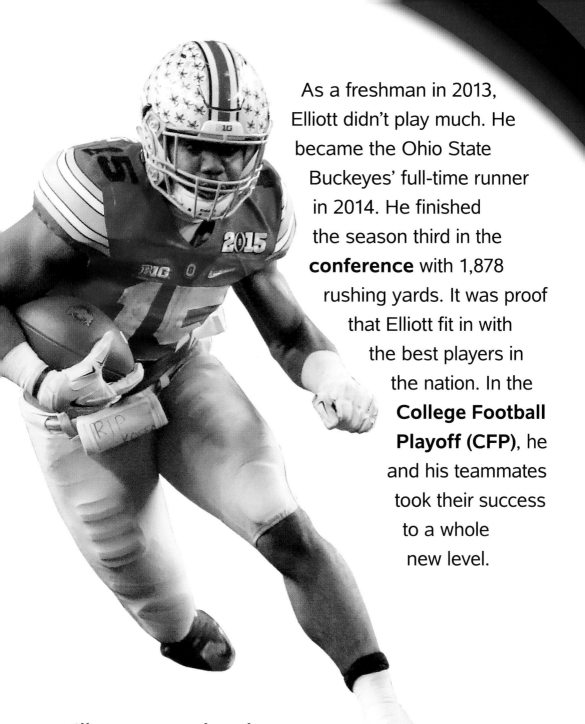

As a freshman in 2013, Elliott didn't play much. He became the Ohio State Buckeyes' full-time runner in 2014. He finished the season third in the **conference** with 1,878 rushing yards. It was proof that Elliott fit in with the best players in the nation. In the **College Football Playoff (CFP)**, he and his teammates took their success to a whole new level.

Elliott competed in the 2015 College Football Playoff.

The winner of the CFP would be the national champion. Many people didn't think Ohio State had a chance against the best teams in the country. But in their first game, Elliott rushed for 230 yards and two touchdowns. Ohio State beat Alabama, 42–35.

Next, the Buckeyes played Oregon for the championship. It was the game that made Elliott a national star. He ran for 246 yards. He also scored four touchdowns. The Buckeyes crushed Oregon, 42–20. "This will go down as one of the great stories in college football history," Ohio State coach Urban Meyer said. Elliott and his teammates were national champions!

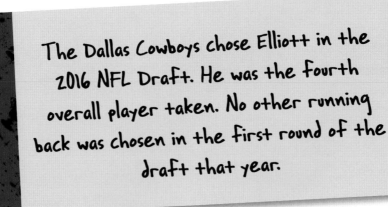

The Dallas Cowboys chose Elliott in the 2016 NFL Draft. He was the fourth overall player taken. No other running back was chosen in the first round of the draft that year.

Elliott ran the hurdles in high school track and field. Now he hurdles over people.

Fans can see it, and NFL players can feel it—Elliott is strong. He's also quick on his feet, graceful, and able to jump right over defenders. He's 6 feet (1.8 m) tall and 225 pounds (102 kg) of pure muscle. How did he get so strong?

As one trainer put it, Elliott is "a beast on the field and in the gym."

During the NFL season, players practice and work out all the time to get ready for games. They start working together before the season even starts. The Cowboys hold team activities in May and June. More intense practices start in July, and games begin in early August. If a team makes it to the **playoffs**, they could be playing all the way until February. When they aren't in season,

Elliott (center) runs drills during Cowboys practices to get ready for games.

it's mostly up to the players to stay in shape.

To get ready for the season, Elliott works with a trainer on his speed and core muscles. Core muscles are in the stomach and back. He targets them with high-intensity interval training (HIIT). During a HIIT session, Elliott works as hard as he can for 30 seconds and then rests for 30 seconds. He does it until he is completely worn out.

Elliott has strong core muscles. Fans can sometimes see his musclar stomach when he is on the sidelines.

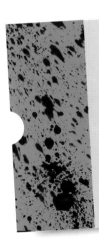

Dallas Cowboys legend Emmitt Smith is the NFL's all-time leader in rushing yards. He knows good running backs, and he's impressed with Ezekiel Elliott. "He's got speed—way more than I ever had," Smith said.

Elliott does a variety of exercises during a HIIT workout. He may ride an exercise bike or do punching drills like a boxer. Sometimes he uses a 50-pound (23 kg) stone. He lifts the stone from the ground and throws it over his shoulder, over and over again. Elliott likes to mix things up and changes his workouts often.

To keep their bodies going, Elliott and his teammates follow a strict diet. Before games or workouts, they eat foods such as pasta and bread that are rich in **carbohydrates**. These foods provide fuel to the body. After games, the players recover with smoothies and meals full of **protein**. Protein helps muscles recover after intense workouts.

Elliott drinks water and sports drinks during games.

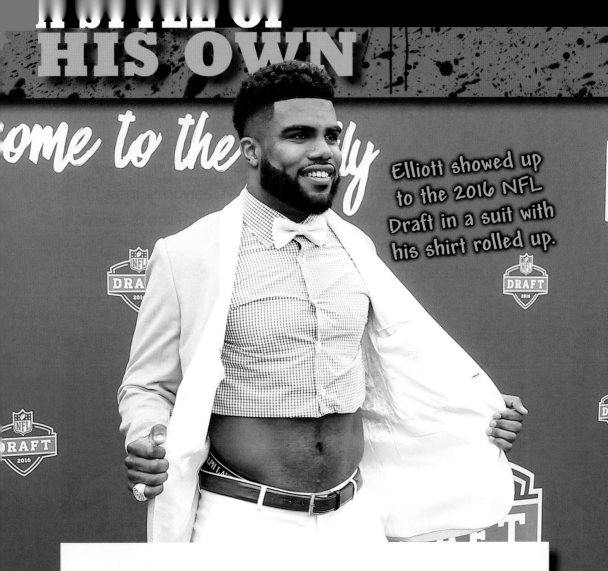

Elliott showed up to the 2016 NFL Draft in a suit with his shirt rolled up.

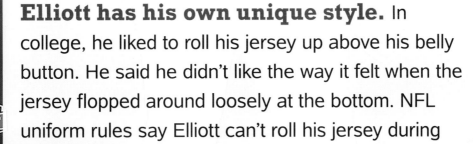

Elliott has his own unique style. In college, he liked to roll his jersey up above his belly button. He said he didn't like the way it felt when the jersey flopped around loosely at the bottom. NFL uniform rules say Elliott can't roll his jersey during

19

Elliott with his shirt rolled up while he is warming up before a game

games anymore, but that doesn't stop him when he's off the field. He even rolled up his shirt to pair with the fancy suit he wore to the NFL Draft.

Elliott's interest in fashion led him to start his own clothing line. The shirts at shopzeke.com are full length, but buyers can roll them up later if they'd like. Fans can also buy hats, hoodies, and other gear.

Another way that Elliott likes to express himself is through body art. He has a huge tattoo of a wolf howling at the moon on his back. He also got a tattoo on his left arm to celebrate Ohio State's national championship. The tattoo shows the Buckeyes' logo, the national championship trophy, and the city of St. Louis.

In 2016, Elliott agreed to a four-year **contract** with the Cowboys that will pay him nearly $25 million.

Elliott's arm tattoo celebrates his team's big win at the CFP.

Elliott's shoes from the December 1, 2016, game

He knows that he's in a great position to give back to his community and help people. He takes part in events with the Salvation Army, such as serving Thanksgiving meals to people in need.

Elliott takes his passion for the cause on the field too. Elliott scored his 13th touchdown of the 2016 season in a game in December. To celebrate, he

Donations to the Salvation Army shot up 61 percent in the day following Elliott's kettle touchdown celebration.

jumped into a huge red kettle on the sideline that the Salvation Army was using to promote their charity efforts. He received a penalty for the celebration, but the move brought a lot of attention to the Salvation Army. Donations to the group shot up after the game, and Elliott gave them $21,000.

COWBOY PRIDE

Elliott carries the ball during the 2017 NFL Pro Bowl.

Elliott has been in the NFL for only a short time, but he has already made a mark. He led the NFL in rushing in 2016 with 1,631 yards. He was voted to his first **Pro Bowl** at the end of the season.

Elliott (*left*) and the Cowboys had a good season in 2016, but losing to the Packers in the playoffs was a disappointment.

The Cowboys had the second-best record in the NFL in 2016. They won 13 games and lost just three. But the team was knocked out of the playoffs by the Green Bay Packers. Quarterback Aaron Rodgers led the Packers to a stunning 34–31 victory.

Elliott had a great season as a **rookie**, but to be a truly great player he has to help his team win in the playoffs. Losing to the Packers was painful for Dallas fans. Elliott took it in stride. He complimented his teammates after the game. He talked about his love for the city of Dallas and how he had found a new home there. Elliott is just getting started in the NFL. He'll have plenty of chances to bring the Super Bowl trophy back to Dallas.

The Dallas Cowboys are one of the most successful teams in NFL history. They've won five Super Bowls, tied for second behind the Pittsburgh Steelers. The Cowboys last won the big game in 1995.

Elliott is proud to be a Cowboy and stands behind his team whether they win or lose.

All-Star Stats

Elliott took the **NFL** by storm in 2016. Leading the league in rushing yards as a rookie was a huge accomplishment. He doesn't have the most rookie rushing yards in **NFL** history though. Take a look at where he ranks on the all-time list.

Most Rushing Yards in a Season by a Rookie

Player	Rushing yards
Eric Dickerson	1,808
George Rogers	1,674
Ezekiel Elliott	1,631
Alfred Morris	1,613
Ottis Anderson	1,605
Edgerrin James	1,553

Source Notes

7   "DAL Ezekiel Elliott Postgame Interview 12.26.16," *Audioboom*, December 27, 2016, https://audioboom.com/posts/5436905-dal -ezekiel-elliott-postgame-interview-12-26-16.

9   Sam Amatuzzo, "Ezekiel Elliott's Epic Quote Should Get Cowboys Fans Amped," *12up*, August 12, 2016, http://www.12up.com/posts /3606280-ezekiel-elliott-s-epic-quote-should-get-cowboys-fans -amped.

11 Laura Amato, "Ezekiel Elliott's Family: The Pictures You Need to See," *Heavy*, April 28, 2016, http://heavy.com/sports/2016/04/ezekiel -elliott-family-dad-stacy-mom-dawn-sisters-instagram-draft-nfl -football-stats-ohio-state-pictures/2.

12 "Elliott Takes Diplomatic Approach When Missouri Is Mentioned," *St. Louis Post-Dispatch*, January 13, 2015, http://www.stltoday.com /sports/college/elliott-takes-diplomatic-approach-when-mizzou-is -mentioned/article_dd3fd2f4-8ceb-5a72-8f88-a2ddec2c1433.html.

14 "Ezekiel Elliott's 4 TDs Lift Ohio State to Inaugural CFP Title over Oregon," *ESPN*, January 13, 2015, http://www.espn.com/college -football/recap?gameId=400610325.

16 Jeff Tomko, "Train Like Running Back Sensation Ezekiel Elliott," *Muscle & Fitness*, accessed April 1, 2017, http://www.muscleandfitness .com/workouts/workout-routines/train-rookie-year-ezekiel-elliott.

17 Charean Williams, "Emmitt Smith Says Ezekiel Elliott Has One Thing He Never Had," *Fort Worth (TX) Star-Telegram*, May 4, 2016, http:// www.star-telegram.com/sports/nfl/dallas-cowboys/article75597682 .html.

Glossary

carbohydrates: substances in foods such as bread and pasta that the body needs to create energy

College Football Playoff (CFP): a tournament held at the end of the season to decide a college football champion

conference: a group of teams that play against one another

contract: an agreement between an athlete and a team that determines a player's salary and time with the team

defensive line: the players who line up before a play at the front of the defense

end zone: the areas at both ends of a football field where touchdowns are scored

heptathlon: a competition that includes seven track-and-field events, such as the long jump and a 200-meter run

interception: a pass that is caught by the defense

linebacker: a player whose main job is to tackle the person with the ball

playoffs: a series of games held to decide a champion

Pro Bowl: a game held each year for the NFL's best players

protein: a substance in foods such as meat and beans that the body needs to build muscles

rookie: a first-year player

Further Information

Dallas Cowboys
http://www.dallascowboys.com

Fishman, Jon M. *Dez Bryant*. Minneapolis: Lerner Publications, 2016.

Football: National Football League
http://www.ducksters.com/sports/national_football_league.php

Mack, Larry. *The Dallas Cowboys Story*. Minneapolis: Bellwether Media, 2017.

NFL RUSH
http://www.nflrush.com

Savage, Jeff. *Aaron Rodgers*. Minneapolis: Lerner Publications, 2012.

Index

Photo Acknowledgments

The images in this book are used with the permission of: Justin K. Aller/Getty Images Sport/Getty Images, p. 1; Tom Pennington/Getty Images Sport/Getty Images, p. 4; Ronald Martinez/Getty Images Sport/Getty Images, pp. 6, 7, 8, 27; Icon Sportswire/Getty Images, p. 9; © John Albright/Icon SMI, p. 10; Henryk Sadura/Shutterstock.com, p. 11; Christian Petersen/Getty Images Sport/Getty Images, p. 12; Ray Carlin/Icon Sportswire/Getty Images, p. 13; Fort Worth Star-Telegram/Tribune News Service/Getty Images, pp. 15, 23; John Green/Cal Sport Media/Alamy Stock Photo, p. 16; Jason Miller/Stringer/Getty Images Sport/Getty Images, p. 17; AP Photo/Ric Tapia/TAPIR, p. 18; Rich Graessle/Icon Sportswire CGV/Newscom, p. 19; Justin K. Aller/Stringer/Getty Images Sport/Getty Images, p. 20; AP Photo/Darron Cummings/ASSOCIATED PRESS, p. 21; Tom Dahlin/Getty Images Sport/Getty Images, p. 22; AP Photo/Jeff Haynes/FR171008 AP/ASSOCIATED PRESS, p. 24; Ezra Shaw/Getty Images Sport/Getty Images, p. 25.

Front cover and design elements: iStock.com/iconeer (gold and silver stars); iStock.com/neyro2008 (motion lines); iStock.com/ulimi (black and white stars); Justin K. Aller/Getty Images Sport/Getty Images (Ezekiel Elliott).